T0131530

A PLACE
WHERE
COMPASSION
IS
CONTRABAND

A PLACE WHERE COMPASSION
IS
CONTRABAND

CHRISTOPHER SEGER

A PLACE WHERE COMPASSION IS CONTRABAND

iUniverse books may be ordered through booksellers or by contacting:

iUniverse
1663 Liberty Drive
Bloomington, IN 47403
www.iuniverse.com
1-800-Authors (1-800-288-4677)

ISBN: 978-1-5320-7731-9 (sc)
ISBN: 978-1-5320-7730-2 (e)

Library of Congress Control Number: 2019908437

Print information available on the last page.

iUniverse rev. date: 06/24/2019

To Jesus Christ, my Lord and Savior,
for without Him I would be nothing

CONTENTS

Acknowledgments ix

Weekend Prison Love 1
Cell-Extraction Christmas 2
The Backstabber 3
The Visitation-Yard Blues 4
Overcoming the 'Stone 5
Dry Snitch 6
Giving It Up For … 7
At Each Other's Throats 8
Death Trap 9
Tears in a Cell Block 10
The Power Freak 11
The Pecking Way 12
Graveyard Love 13
Craving Attention 14
Easy Money 15
A Sexual Cesspool 16
Being a Pup at Limestone 17
Sack Lunch from Heaven 18
Insignificant 19
Limestone Time 20
Alabama Tax Code 21
Deep Thoughts from a Pond 22
Lonesome at the 'Stone 23
Simple Minds 24
Fellow Officer in Blue 25

Alabama Julip 26

Pill-Call Prayer 27

White-Boy Rap 28

The LT's World 29

The Snitch 30

Shakedown Shack Rap 31

Limestone Rap 32

Seg Unit 33

B-Side Shift Office 34

Another Inmate Bucking 35

Slap Down 36

A CO's B-Side Blues 37

10 Dorm 38

The Cement 39

Prison Jeopardy 40

Jesus Is My Cell Mate 41

Parlay Board in My Mind 42

Inmate Blues 43

Pure Evil 44

Luke and the AIDS Death Trap 45

A Black and White Thing 46

The Constant Need 47

Public Safety 48

The Double H 49

Part-Timer 50

O Captain, My Captain 51

Flatbed 52

A Heart's Desire 53

About the Author 55

ACKNOWLEDGMENTS

This book would not be possible without the support of friends, family, and peers. Thanks to all of you.

To April and Spot, who were there for the trials and tribulations of the Department of Corrections.

To Anthony Roper, who showed me that your family always comes first in life.

To Dewayne Estes, who sat me down and explained what Corrections was really all about.

Jimmy Patrick was always ready to support me in my efforts for a better firing range, a real leader.

Braderick Files, with a quick smile and an attitude to help in any way I needed.

Thanks also to Juan Bailey, Ricky Smith, and Laura Stisher, who toil daily in the mysteries of the mind and mental health. Juan showed me that we are all human and our flaws make us who we are.

To the substance-abuse team, who fight the good battle between the demons of addiction and the light of clean living.

Mitch Coady, we laughed and cried over the years. Thanks for the great homemade meals. James Smith, your clarity of mind and calm demeanor helped me work in the craziness of the prison world. Thanks to Dad, Mom, George, Maddie, Nancy, Mary Lou, and Claire—the greatest family ever.

To my Alabama family—Ella Rae, Willow Grace, Wil, Kate, Chas, Tara, Regina, Charley, Rhonda, Gerritt, Willie, and Linda—you all are great blessings from God.

WEEKEND PRISON LOVE

They all line up in the early-morning hours,
With love in their eyes and coins enough to fill the towers.
Every weekend each woman comes up to see her man,
So during the week he can work on his new tan.
They will cut in front of each other every time
And are quick to snitch and drop a dime.
The convicts will cry and spill a tale of need,
And the women's hearts glow—but not aware of the greed.
I search all the vehicles from heaven to Sodom
To make sure their boyfriends do not try to his in the bottom.
They keep coming back, searching for love lost,
And the phone bills drive up the cost.
Once the inmate gets out, now the fun begins,
To deal with him every day and realize what a mistake it's been.

CELL-EXTRACTION CHRISTMAS

We all lined up, one in front of the other,
Waiting for Sarge's word to get another.
I had the leg irons, and one had the stun gun,
So we could all have some fun.
Two more jumped in
To make sure we wouldn't commit any SOP sins.
Sarge lit up the shock shield to everyone's surprise.
It said "Merry Christmas" before our eyes.
The inmate stood on top of his bunk,
Waiting to be the ultimate punk.
We got him on his belly to get the restraints poised,
When all of a sudden, there was a loud noise.
Santa Claus appeared outside the cell,
Just stopping by for a spell.
He said, "Hello, officers. I was doing a fence check
When I heard the clatter
Of an inmate releasing his bladder.
There will be no sweets for this inmate,
Too crazy for any cell mate."
He told the cell-extraction team to keep up the good works
Because the lieutenant wanted all the perks.
The reindeer got ready to leave when Saint Nick blessed all of us
And wished as a great New Year.

(For C. B. Thanks.)

THE BACKSTABBER

He drives to work with all smiles,
Ready to stick you with a knife as long as a mile.
By keeping it always in an uproar,
The supervisors will shake their heads like a big bore.
All he has been through, it still comes back,
Time and again, like a hungry wolf pack.
The devil is using him with all his might,
So he is blinded by Satan's sight.
The spirit of division is what keeps him going
Because payback will be hell from everyone
who has gotten a hard boning.

THE VISITATION-YARD BLUES

Every weekend, the families start to come up the road.
They are all excited about seeing their loved
ones while carrying a hard load.
I have to process them in, one at a time,
Never knowing which one is bringing in the nickel dime.
When everyone gets settled on the patio,
Husbands and wives will kiss and hug, plus the
kids play with their new daddy-o.
I have to be on the lookout for any obscene moves,
Because when it gets hot and heavy, no one wants to get booed.
Girlfriends spend all their change at the little store,
While the inmate eats his way down to the core.
Marriages are made here, promises given with a lot of tender lace,
And they make sure to give each other a lot of space.
They try to beat us on any given Sunday,
But the drug dogs are out, and it's their fun day.
As the prison years go by, the loved ones will kick the inmate to the curb
Because driving up to the prison gets old and
dangerous, trying to smuggle some herb.

OVERCOMING THE 'STONE

No matter what is thrown at me,
I know in my heart that God will always be.
The Bible says to be baptized with water
So you can see the light and do what's right—sorta.
It's all about inviting Jesus into your life
So you can start to walk on the inside like a kite.
The spiritual journey that is your life now
Will not end with the grave.
This life is only preparation for the one to come,
When we can be united with God the Father for all eternity.
Never reject Him or His Word,
Because when that knee bows down,
All will confess that Christ is Lord.

(To Norm Webb Sr., a true man of God.)

DRY SNITCH

It's a habit some pick up in the camp,
When you can't stop and not turn on the lamp.
A very dangerous way to live for a liar,
Always looking for someone to bring the fire.
That is when the powers up above unleash a bit.
It strikes a hand like a baton hit.
One day it will come full circle for you,
And then your eyes will open and see an ocean of blue.
When you destroy other lives for fun,
It will surprise you when you face the gun.

GIVING IT UP FOR ...

Just when I could not take it anymore,
The devil came to me with a little folklore.
He said, "Let your manhood go for a bag of cookies,"
And he would protect me from the other bookies.
I agreed and did the dirty deed,
Without thinking of its future devilish creed.
When people call you a sissy,
They don't understand it's enough to make you dizzy.
Never thought it would come to this
When I was raising hell and stealing in bliss.
Brought a lot of shame and pain to my family's side.
Now it has come full circle to my backside.
I regret what I did in my youth
Because now I'm someone's property for a pair of boots.
Gave it up for a cup of noodles,
And here I sit, being someone's poodle.

AT EACH OTHER'S THROATS

You can feel it in the prison air,
When you walk through the front gate into the lion's lair.
Everybody in blue stares at each other real hard,
Hoping to catch someone moving like a lard.
It happens when you least expect it.
One day all smiles, the next day—
The rope bit.
Looking for people abusing sick leave
So the higher-ups can start the paperwork weave.
Words start to fly at the drop of a hat.
The phone calls begin so someone can go to the mat.
Once the warden is involved, it's all over.
The union won't stop; it just act like a "little rover."
And now you have no job to go to
Because someone got in your face and you did not sue.

DEATH TRAP

It's just a little shack by the side of the road,
And when trouble starts, it's no one's abode.
The day begins with a cold snap.
After a time, it feels like running a lap.
I try to stop unauthorized folks from coming in
So the higher-ups do not get mad and start to sin.
Anyone can take a shot at me.
That's why I wear a vest, you see.
Some people help me out with a lot of good advice,
Because when the guns go off, everyone gets really nice.

TEARS IN A CELL BLOCK

I started with a great outlook.
Then I realized the prison was no schoolbook.
During the academy, it was all one work,
But in the camp, it was backstabbing with a real dirk.
To my surprise, it was just me and my radio sound.
After the pepper spray was done, the tears in
the cell block started with no pun.
My last vision was blue running away,
So I pray my runner will save my day.

THE POWER FREAK

He says he wants it all
And will have everyone standing tall.
When it comes time to bark orders,
That is where he has no borders.
Whatever it takes is the rule of the day,
So when the heat is on, it is only his say.
It's an addiction all the way through,
One that will have people running in a wild zoo.
The power freak will go on and on
Because everybody is too scared to speak to the don.
He really does not run anything; it's all in his head.
When the grim reaper taps on his shoulder,
he will awaken in the devil's bed.

THE PECKING WAY

When power enters a person's heart,
It does things that make verbal darts.
They think the Word turns on them,
Never realizing that it's God's own gem.
The flesh will creep in and talk,
So eyes will open up and balk.
Everyone has their place, they say,
As long as no one bothers them for more pay.
One day, the Master will call,
And all their power will fall.

GRAVEYARD LOVE

She was just another woman, looking for a job,
And thought the prison would be like working at Bob's.
The inmate saw her walk in with a smile.
He knew then it would be like walking a mile.
When she started talking to the convict, it felt real lame,
One day all love, the next the old game.
The inmate pulled out his best con trick,
And she fell hook, line, and sinker, as quick as a Bic.
Now she sees him every weekend to be his sacrificial lamb
And spends all her money on his crooked scam.

CRAVING ATTENTION

I came up to the prison to find someone.
The inmate started to talk like it would be a lot of fun.
All his attention was on me.
It helps a girl out, don't you see?
Now he wants to get out and move in,
But it's moving too fast to be someone's next of kin.
His drug problems have never been confronted.
So it's like being on a baseball field and having bunted.
Where will this romance end up to?
When the con games start, it makes me feel blue.
Someone in white has nothing to really offer,
Like my last man, who hit me until I looked like a brown coffer.
I hope from one relationship to another,
One day I will find a true lover.

EASY MONEY

They call it easy money for some,
But I know I work like it's never done.
A lot of blue come in and say with a smile,
"It's just another day to fake break by a mile."
The state pays a lot of taxpayer money out,
So the lazy ones can come in and always pout.
When will it end? No one really knows.
Some quit and try to get a job at Joe Blow's.
Many come back realizing how good it was with all their might.
Then they vow never to leave and start to sweat
when they see the warden's light.

A SEXUAL CESSPOOL

I thought working in an HCU was a lot of fun.
But then the officers started to look at me with eyes like a gun.
Being a little female at a prison is not fair.
All day long, the men in blue want to take me to their lair.
They constantly get in my space
While I'm trying not to spray them with their own mace.
The phone calls at night get real old,
When all I hear is heavy breathing and a promise of gold.
I pray that it will stop one day,
But the sexual cesspool is as large as limestone bay.

BEING A PUP AT LIMESTONE

All my street homies looked at my messed-up life,
And all I could think of was another hit from the pipe.
Horse-playing and grabbing butt fill my day,
But I always know when it's time to pay.
My innocent mind brought down by my plight,
Tricked out of my manhood by my mere fright.
Every day the officer comes around and tells me to grab a pail
Because all night long it was me bent over the handrail.
Looking back on the people that I messed over,
Just wishing I could turn it around and stop being someone's rover.
Shaved all my hairs off my body,
And now I have a new name for my hobby.
Wearing Daisy Dukes all the time,
Getting ready to drop the dime.
Being called a gangster ho by all,
Even the police treat me like a flat basketball.
Once I get out, I will act like a man
And try to live down all I did in the can.

SACK LUNCH FROM HEAVEN

Every day I check out to cut more grass,
And I work with all my might to make sure it will pass.
The boss man lets me smoke a little every now and then.
But when his whistle blows, I know it's time to crack and bend.
When it got toward lunchtime, to everyone's surprise,
Instead of kitchen slop, we looked up with our eyes.
Sack lunches were falling everywhere from heaven,
And they dropped with a thud, so we knew they weren't leaven.
The boss man started to laugh and smile,
And said, "You all are blessed today from heaven by a mile."
We all ran around and opened the bags.
Inside were a full-course meal and a note with a tag.
The note said, "From your heavenly Father,
who loves you with his might.
So eat 'til your stomach is full, and treat the officers right."

(To M. P.)

INSIGNIFICANT

It's tough working in cement stone every day,
Always knowing you will never get another say.
When you ask the higher-ups for a favor,
It's a feeling they know you will never savor.
To be insignificant and not worth a look
Make you want to go buy a law book.
Upper management does not really care
As long as you stay calm and act like a teddy bear.
No matter what the issue is, the glazed look in the eyes
Let's you know that it is time for the lies.
For the convict, they will do cartwheels.
But if you wear blue, you will not get a state meal.
So sit back and relax because your phone call will be treated like Ex-Lax.
Never will they get back to you,
So get used to feeling like you are in the "Blue."

LIMESTONE TIME

Day in, day out, everything is the same,
But you only have yourself to blame.
Stealing, robbing, and killing is your game.
Now you have a number in front of your name.
Learn from your mistakes; don't make them twice.
Or for the rest of your life, it's patties and rice.

ALABAMA TAX CODE

In the land of cotton and peaches,
There is a tax code that is full of leeches.
All the legislature who say they're Christian
Have the power to change it but move as slow as a piston.
It punishes the poor with unfair weights,
While timberland goes for a dollar an acre at the gates.
The special interest groups and their paid cronies
Work hard to get money for a lobbyist, Tony.
Property taxes are the lowest in the nation.
Nothing changes as they go on another vacation.
But God is watching over the Deep South,
And judgment day will come and fix it no doubt.
And when they stand in Montgomery before God
To answer why they treasured their sod,
So they will go into the lake of fire.
All because they sold themselves to big money hires.

DEEP THOUGHTS FROM A POND

Standing here on my post, ready for another day,
Wishing it was sometime in May.
Smelling the waste from the inmates' butts,
It goes down my lungs and out my guts.
Wondering why did Sarge put me in this shack?
Somehow I think it is a large payback.
Watching all the employees drive in with a rush,
Never stopping to see who is the real lush.
Waving at all the people I meet,
Hoping that I will not have to speak.
They look at every move that I make,
So my gun won't put them in the lake.
It gets hotter and hotter by the hour,
And I start to feel real sour.
Waiting for my relief to turn on a dime,
Knowing that Big H is never on time.

LONESOME AT THE 'STONE

Each and every night, I sleep on my rack.
That's when all the sissies come out to play a little blackjack.
Wondering why I put myself in this hell,
Waiting for the officer in the cube to click my cell.
My cellie and me we fight like cats and dogs,
But when his store is called, we become like two hogs.
I bum Black & Milds all day,
And the coffee I get is not from eBay.
I'm just a little white boy, still scared after all these years,
Never knowing when will I become a sissy and cry a lot of tears.
I have not learned all my lessons yet
Because I keep coming back on a bet.
I'm really tired of doing all this time,
But I really like to snitch folks out on a dime.
So here I stay with all my friends,
Always knowing I am not really making amends.

SIMPLE MINDS

I used to work at a day care with kids.
Now it's a state prison with adults and short lids.
Trying to get my job done in a professional way,
But the supervisors with no backbone have no say.
Most of the officers cry all the time
Because all they will get are days off and a fine.
It's like having grown babies all around you;
Sometimes it makes me feel real blue.
When will they grow up? No one knows.
It's all about retirement and a cold one to go.

FELLOW OFFICER IN BLUE

We all go through the same academy—
All shiny and ready to do our duty.
Now in the prison camp, it's all about who is covering your booty.
When your personal problems get you down,
Don't take it out on me and dog me like a hound.
When the supervisor wants to write you up and run you out,
I'm putting food on my family's table, without a doubt.
I come to work every day with a smile on my face.
I don't expect your troubled face in my space.
When your blood pressure starts kicking in,
I'll be at your funeral, saluting you, without that grin—
Not that inmate who you treated like gold;
He shanked you, and now you've grown cold.
I'll look at your family and their grief.
They will lay you in the ground, and the funeral will cease.
I pray, Lord, that I can get some relief.

ALABAMA JULIP

Named after a southern drink to make you happy,
Inmates cook it to make them feel sappy.
We are constantly looking for it all over the camp,
Only to find it under the captain's lamp.
Convicts will hoard it during the holiday season
So they can drink it for any old reason.
Many inmates drink it with glee.
It wouldn't be bad if they could only see.
Smells like a dirty pair of drawers,
So when you walk in the dorm, you have to watch your pores.
When we find it, it's usually in plastic jugs,
And we'll take it to the shift office to check for bugs.
The correctional officers do their best to track it down,
And the inmates make sure they are never around.

PILL-CALL PRAYER

Standing in a line that never seems to bend,
It's called pill call, but to what end?
Pushing the meds down our throats,
Waiting for the right amount to float.
Hoping one day the fences will come down
Because the nurses just never seem to be around.

WHITE-BOY RAP

Got caught messing up in a dorm.
Don't know when I'm going to get in form.
Trying to pay off the items I owe,
Hoping I won't become someone's ho.
Scared all the time, just trying to survive,
Waiting for Officer Friendly to help me get by.
Thank God it's chow call so I can eat.
I'm tired of just listening to a beat.
The gangbangers tried to get in my cell box,
But they don't know I'm quick as a fox.
I'm just a white boy trying to stay intact,
With all my buddies waiting to get in my sack.
Being outnumbered is a new experience,
One that has helped me become delirious.
I will get out one day,
But I'm starting to like it, so I just might stay.

THE LT'S WORLD

In a world where she carries a telescope,
Constantly looking for another dorm to put under the microscope,
It's like a magic show, where everyone is catching out.
But when push comes to shove,
It's just another day to pout.
When the captain hollers, everything comes to a halt,
Especially when it's time to see who is at fault.
Ranting and raving, it's a lot of the job,
To let your officers know when they need to get
On the knob.
The paperwork is overwhelming,
Even when you have a shift clerk
Who does a lot of telling.
Shift after shift, the office is always a safe haven,
So you can know who needs some positive shaving.
Working the sissies with a lot of passion
For the big ho down under hand bashing.

THE SNITCH

He is despised by all
But used like a battering ball.
Always ready to spill his guts,
Just depending on who has got him by the nuts.
Will tell on his own sister, Mandy,
Just for another piece of candy.
His words are treated like gold,
Especially when it comes to a CO he told.
Wardens come down to listen to his wild tales
So they can get another on the bucket detail.
Sometimes he's wired; sometimes he's not.
Watch out for his marked money; it will save you a lot.
Can wear blue or white,
It doesn't matter as long as he gets his next bite.

SHAKEDOWN SHACK RAP

In a little building by the Mexican jail
Is where hope finally comes to a nail.
For all who wear white
Will take off their clothes, so we don't have to fight.
Some inmates try to get something by.
They don't realize it's all just a lie
Because the officer quietly checks all their pockets,
To see if there are any loose lockets.
I help out with all my might
To try to find just where is the cigarette light.
We work till all the squads are in.
Then it's back to trade school rover, where it all begins.
Inmate runners have the most up-to-date out-gate debts,
Along with the latest slick pick bets.
It all works smoothly till second shift comes up with a new deck.
Then it's to the house for a nice cold longneck.

LIMESTONE RAP

Some drama kicked off in the gym today.
Little did they know this place was gonna pay,
Doing whatever it takes to stay on top.
But all my homeboys just wanna kick the slop.
Sweating the sissies day after day,
Until it all comes down to a blade.
Lying on my bed in a place called the parking lot,
Trying to figure out where all the traffic stopped.
Hemmed up, stopped up till a man breaks,
That's when you know what you can take.
Being a man is tough at the stone
Because it's all about slipping the bone.

SEG UNIT

In a place where there is no beer,
It's all about taking it in the rear.
They call it the dungeon, where the regulator lives.
Every once in a while, he gives.
His gloves and talk keep us in luck
From those who want to buck.
The house of pain will never end
As long as there is inmates who will lend.
Day after day, I hear the screams
Of young men who face their dreams.
When will they learn to just get along,
Stop fighting, and listen to another song?

B-SIDE SHIFT OFFICE

In a room where decisions are made,
Affecting everyone who crosses the slade,
LT waits for the first inmate of the day
Who opens his mouth to protest his cell mate.
She puts all in check wearing blue and white.
If you don't believe it, just call light.
The sarge is there when all else fails
For a therapy that has hurt many tails.
I do all the necessary talking,
Especially for those who do the stalking.
Also be there to help the CO's pout
For all the ones who have an out.
They all come together to do their eight
With pride and courage till the next gate.

ANOTHER INMATE BUCKING

I walked into the dorm just wanting him to see the light,
When all of a sudden, he told me to take a hike.
They called it bucking in this world full of men.
All it really comes down to is me using my pen.
I pulled out my baton with a lot of ease,
Plus my pepper spray worked just as I please.
The inmate said, "Okay, I will go to work.
Just don't treat me like a jerk."
He said he was sorry for disrespecting me so.
I told him, "Make sure it doesn't happen
again, or we will have another go."
He was escorted to HCU very slowly,
While the pepper spray worked on him and brought him lowly.
Processed into 9 dorm was the next stop.
Once in the cell, he cried and said
His lawyer's name was Attorney Crissie.
Then I knew he would always be a little sissy.

SLAP DOWN

They call it slap down, and that's what it is
When a man meets a sissy,
And her name is Miss Lissie.
One man's eyes are down on the ground.
The other is looking up and slamming him around.
Some call it getting some straighten.
It's what inmates stew,
If people know what the CO could really do.
When one inmate owes another and he tries to duck,
He will always end up getting bucked.

A CO'S B-SIDE BLUES

In a place where supervisors are always looking for you to fail,
It helps a lot when you can get some tail.
B-side used to be a quiet area with a lot of hugs,
Now it's a Babylon cesspool full of thugs.
CO to CO, we are always supposed to look out for each other.
But when the higher-ups come around, it's all about getting some cover.
Never knowing when the paperwork will fall,
Just trying to make a dime and stand up tall.
Every morning you have to deal with all these knuckleheads,
Just trying to get them to make up their beds.
Supervisors jumping to conclusions become very time consuming,
But when your neck is in the noose, your head starts swooning.
Gangsters, mentally ill, and perverts fill my day.
I can take it as long as I get some pay.
Praying one day I will leave Limestone.
Hopefully it won't be named after me on my tombstone.

10 DORM

The schemer, the scammer, and the master manipulator,
Always running from the real regulator.
He looks to see who is in the cube,
Then he will decide if it is safe to run a tube.
When he comes in your dorm,
All hell is about to be born.
The Bates Motel in all its gory,
Is just like 10 dorm in all its glory.
Egos and pride fall to the wayside,
In a place where all is thrown to the curbside.
Inmates short and inmates tall,
No matter; this dorm is always ready for another fall.
Sissies are made every day.
It will never stop until someone gets his pay.
They call it 10 dorm; it's where I make my dime,
Hoping to God I never come to dine.

THE CEMENT

I work in a path of gravel and stone.
I work in places most people have never known.
Eyes of evil around me all day long,
Long stares of hatred, some not so visible shone.
You'll show me no mercy if you shine a shank at my side.
So I am watchful as I walk and listen to your lies.
I am here on this gravel and stone cement home for eight hours a day.
I've come to realize that it is not worth the pay.

PRISON JEOPARDY

You thought it was just another game to play.
Now it's up to you to say yes or nay.
You have to answer the question with a question.
There are a lot of convicts all looking for a session.
Your fellow officers are looking out for no one but themselves,
So don't press the wrong button, or else.
And when the game is over and everyone goes home,
It will start all over again as high as the capitol dome.
So be careful what happens when your back is turned
Because prison jeopardy will be ready to get you burned.

JESUS IS MY CELL MATE

My eyes open wide on the top bunk.
It is another day in the state prison, smelling the funk.
But Jesus is changing the tide
To protect me from my demon side.
When Satan tries to talk a pitch,
He is looking to put me in a clinch.
Here comes Jesus, and the Antichrist dies—
Plus Lucifer takes off around the corner with his lies.
It is great to have a Son of God in my house.
That's when all the evil is quiet as a mouse.
I am trying to be good with no bugs.
Just hope JC will not find my drugs.

PARLAY BOARD IN MY MIND

As I look at the new rookies coming through the door,
I wonder which one will last and not hit the floor.
The days go by and lips start to talk,
And the fingers point to see who will be bought.
Human weakness starts to show up,
And the inmate tricksters will be ready to sup.
One day the warden will call the officer to his room
To show him his ways of doom.
Another fresh parlay board goes up in my mind
As I see a bunch of eager new finds.

INMATE BLUES

You come in the dorm and hide in the bathroom with ease,
Thinking you can do as you please.
When you pull the nasty deed out,
It makes the whole dorm laugh with a snout.
It's a sickness of the mind they say,
Always waiting for another female officer to look your way.
When you get to 9 dorm, the game is over
Because the payback is in full force with the rover.
The bruises heal slowly with time,
And you will remember how you got snitched out for a dime.

PURE EVIL

There is a place where the inferno lives on,
A special circle of hell, where it's one big con.
All forms of perversion thrive and grow.
It's a state prison, where inmates act real low.
The petri dish of pure evil spreads and multiplies,
Like a virus and germ in which both satisfies.
The dirty deeds here are all done with pleasure.
So the beasts of flesh have a lot of tattoos to measure.
But the screams of the innocent are lost forever,
And the scales of justice tip with a crooked lever.

LUKE AND THE AIDS DEATH TRAP

It starts with a long, hard stare.
Then the unnatural acts begin to bare.
Grown men doing what God says makes him puke,
Bringing disease and death to an inmate named Luke.
At night in the dorms and in the cells,
You can hear the screams pitch out like a loud bell.
The blood comes out with a death trap,
And Luke ends up in the hospital in a blanket wrap.
The death scene is not very nice.
The inmate closes his eyes and waits for the roll of the dice.

A BLACK AND WHITE THING

Don't let it be a black and white thing, brother,
Because it just stops the love of a mother.
The devil sits back and laughs all day
As we hate each other, no matter what we say.
It's just a trick that he uses with glee,
And we fall for it every time, like a cup of tea.
Just read the Bible, and you will see.
That is when your eyes can look up and be like me.
Racism is a dead-end trip.
All it will lead us to is a long hell's slip.
We are a team of blue; never forget the truth.
So it's sink or swim in the same prison cubicle booth.

THE CONSTANT NEED

Working in a prison is tough,
Never knowing when the inmates will bluff.
Walking into a cell block full of hate,
I just hope I don't come in late.
It begins with an inmate's con game,
Just to see if I will be real lame.
The hardest part is not all the time,
But when the supervisors smile and tell a little line.
Backstabbing and snitching are parts of the game.
Waiting for retirement, so I can move to Maine.
Locking up folks is what I do.
I am not ashamed, just asking for my due.

PUBLIC SAFETY

They say I violate an inmate's rights
When I tell one to work and see the light.
I use force to help me out,
And then the inmates run and pout.
If the lawyers get involved, it is not pretty,
Especially in court, when the jury looks with pity.
My job is to keep them in line,
So they will not break into your house sign.
The state will back me up all the way
Because it is public safety and another day.

THE DOUBLE H

I walked into a place called the Double H
With my girl at my side, looking for a quiet place.
All I saw was tormented souls,
Each one drinking, and crying was their goals.
The demon spirits were all around,
Waiting to pounce on the next round.
The walls were soaked with misery and pain
Of people before who never gained.
The lady at the front door takes your money,
And with a crooked smile and bad breath says, "Hello, honey."
Hell is never filled and always coping,
Just like the Double H, whose door never stops swinging open.
As we left a chill went down my spine.
The head devil in the band said, "Come back. Let's talk and dine."

PART-TIMER

I'm just a part-timer, looking for a check.
Will work day or night with no rest.
With a lot of experience and time.
It really does not mean anything, just some dimes.
My old body can still work all the dorms,
Just like a rookie, only slower, but still the norm.
I try to tell the new COs how to work a snitch,
But they say, "Pop, just sit down before you trip."
I think I'll work 'til Social Security kicks in,
So you can find me in a casino, praying for forgiveness of my sins.

O CAPTAIN, MY CAPTAIN

It started with a dad who treated him bad.
So he felt like a small child and very sad.
Working in the camp with inmates around,
They did whatever he said with no sound.
When he got the power, he wanted everyone to kiss his ring,
Having people serve him like he was a king.
When I had to sit and wait for him to eat,
I knew then he was a narcissist marching to his own beat.
It was humiliating and demoralizing to be around him,
Never knowing when it would end with me losing a limb.
"I was just doing my job," he would say.
But I knew that it was a lie and waited for the day.
It was like a weight lifting from my shoulders when he retired.
I realized then I would never be fired.
And so my life begins with new sight.
With Jesus by my side, I see the light.

FLATBED

They call me Flatbed; that's my name,
With a bottle of pills and a dummy log with no one to blame.
A girl is in my coach bed, waiting for me to hit another mile.
I just hope I keep this hard smile.
Truck stops come and go, and all look the same,
Some real wild, others too tame.
The road is my home for now,
So I can get my check and hit the town.

(For Willie South.)

A HEART'S DESIRE

I fell in love with a convict today.
Everyone said he would treat me in a new way.
The DON told me it would cost me my job,
But I still love that inmate's nob.
He makes my heart glow,
So he can bring me down real low.
Whatever he wants me to do, I will,
And that means a cell phone and lots of dollar bills.
I'm just an LPN with no future.
I hope my man in white will stop mooching.
One day he will be free and start taking care of me.
Until then, I will bend over and smile for him, you see.
The wall of shame does not scare me at all.
My heart wants to be at that inmate's beck and call.

ABOUT THE AUTHOR

Christopher Seger has been a correctional lieutenant with the Alabama Department of Corrections (ALDOC) for more than twenty-five years. Previously working at the Louisiana State Prison in Angola helped him deal with the inmate subculture. Each poem has a story behind it and reflects what it is like to work in a prison world. Working on the inside can impact a person's outlook on life and other people. This is his first book, with others on the way.

Printed in the United States
By Bookmasters